# FBI AGENT

## By Geoffrey M. Horn

**Reading Consultant:** Susan Nations, M.Ed.,
author/literacy coach/consultant in literacy development

**Gareth Stevens**
Publishing

Please visit our web site at **www.garethstevens.com.**
For a free catalog describing Gareth Stevens Publishing's list of high-quality books,
call 1-800-542-2595 (USA) or 1-800-387-3178 (Canada).
Gareth Stevens Publishing's fax: 1-877-542-2596

**Library of Congress Cataloging-in-Publication Data**
Horn, Geoffrey M.
     FBI agent / by Geoffrey M. Horn.
       p. cm. — (Cool careers : helping careers)
     Includes bibliographical references and index.
     ISBN-10: 0-8368-9193-7    ISBN-13: 978-0-8368-9193-5 (lib. bdg.)
     ISBN-10: 0-8368-9326-3    ISBN-13: 978-0-8368-9326-7 (softcover)
     1. United States. Federal Bureau of Investigation—Vocational
guidance—Juvenile literature.  I. Title.
     HV8144.F43H67   2008
     363.250973—dc22                          2008010380

This edition first published in 2009 by
**Gareth Stevens Publishing**
A Weekly Reader® Company
1 Reader's Digest Rd.
Pleasantville, NY 10570-7000 USA

Copyright © 2009 by Gareth Stevens, Inc.

Senior Managing Editor: Lisa M. Herrington
Editor: Joann Jovinelly
Creative Director: Lisa Donovan
Designer: Paula Jo Smith
Photo Researcher: Kimberly Babbitt

**Picture credits:** Cover, title page: Shawn Thew/epa/Corbis; p. 5 Newscom; p. 6 Robyn
Beck/AFP/Getty Images; p. 7 Zuma/Newscom; pp. 8–9 © Greg Smith/Corbis; p. 10 ©
William Whitehurst/Corbis; p. 11 © Bettmann/Corbis; p. 12 © Greg Smith/Corbis; p. 15
Dorling Kindersley/Getty Images; p. 16 Laurie J. Bennett; p. 17 (top) © George Steinmetz/
Corbis; p. 17 (bottom) © Bettmann/Corbis; p. 18 © Anna Clopet/Corbis; p. 19 Steve Rouse/
AP Images; pp. 20, 22, 23 © Anna Clopet/Corbis; p. 24 Time Life Pictures/Getty Images; p.
25 Roberto Schmidt/AFP/Getty Images; p. 26 Jerry Hoefer/AP Images; p. 28 Mark Wilson/
Getty Images

Printed in the United States of America

1 2 3 4 5 6 7 8 9 10 09 08

# CONTENTS

Words in the glossary appear in **bold** type the first time they are used in the text.

# CHAPTER 1

# ON THE CASE

A spy sells American defense secrets to Russia. A congressman takes bribes and stuffs the money in his home freezer. A baseball player cheats by using illegal drugs. A gunman wearing a ski mask robs a series of Chicago banks. **Terrorists** plot to blow up an airport in Los Angeles.

What do these real-life events have in common? These are the kinds of cases that **FBI** agents investigate.

## What the FBI Does

FBI stands for Federal Bureau of Investigation. The FBI is a U.S. government agency. FBI agents solve crimes and enforce laws. They also protect Americans from terrorists and foreign spies.

The FBI is not a national police force. It does not investigate all crimes. Local police enforce local laws. These are laws that apply only in a particular city or town. State police enforce state laws. These are laws that apply only in a particular state.

The FBI works with local and state police. It also works with police groups in foreign countries. But its main job is to enforce federal laws. These are laws that apply to the entire country.

FBI agents seize evidence from the home of a man accused of spying for Russia.

The FBI may take over a local case when federal laws have been broken. For example, local or state police handle most murder cases. But if a **serial killer** is involved, the FBI may take the case. The FBI always deals with plots to harm the nation or its leaders.

## Who Works for the FBI?

The FBI has more than 30,000 employees. More than 12,000 of them are special agents. Agents carry out investigations. They collect **evidence**. They question witnesses. They arrest people suspected of breaking the law.

Agents in riot gear deal with a hostage situation in Los Angeles, California.

Some FBI agents have more unusual tasks. For example, the FBI has **hostage** rescue teams. Their job is to save people who have been captured by terrorists or other criminals. The FBI even has scuba teams. These agents are expert divers. They recover evidence from rivers, lakes, and harbors. They also check piers and ships for underwater bombs.

About 18,000 other people work for the FBI. They help the agents do their jobs. Many of these workers have special skills. Some are good at science or computers. Others are excellent at foreign languages.

# Is This the Right Career for You?

Do you like reading crime and mystery stories? Are you interested in police work? Do you enjoy solving puzzles? Are you good at asking questions? If so, a career as an FBI agent may be the right choice for you. As an FBI agent, you can help people by stopping crime. You can help protect the United States from its enemies. You can help enforce the law. You can work to make sure that lawbreakers get punished.

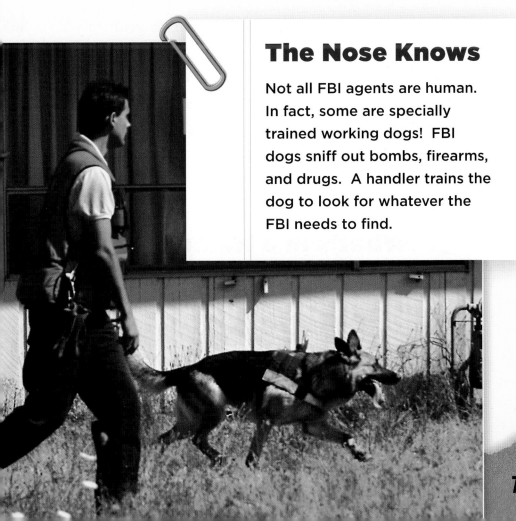

## The Nose Knows

Not all FBI agents are human. In fact, some are specially trained working dogs! FBI dogs sniff out bombs, firearms, and drugs. A handler trains the dog to look for whatever the FBI needs to find.

# CHAPTER 2

# WHAT DO FBI AGENTS DO?

What is a typical day like for an FBI agent? "No day is ever the same," says an FBI agent named Dina. "You never know what challenge or opportunity you may be offered next. Have your passport ready because you could be on a plane flying to Paris to interview a person of interest. You could assist another office and conduct **surveillance** operations in their division. If that's not exciting enough, how about putting the cuffs on a **notorious** crime figure?"

## What's in a Name?

The FBI's name has changed three times since it was founded in 1908.

| | |
|---|---|
| 1908 | Founded as "special agent force" |
| 1909 | Bureau of Investigation |
| 1932 | United States Bureau of Investigation |
| 1935 | Federal Bureau of Investigation |

FBI agents go through a target training exercise in Dallas, Texas.

Since President Theodore Roosevelt formed the special agent force in 1908, agents like Dina have been trained to be federal crime fighters. Roosevelt thought government could solve crimes by using experts. He wanted to fight crime by putting together a team of special agents who would be well trained and well disciplined. They would become experts in their field. Today, FBI agents investigate crimes that range from spying to computer fraud.

At a crime scene, many kinds of evidence are collected, photographed, and labeled.

# Criminal Investigations

Today's agents must be highly trained. They also have to be science experts. All agents must be familiar with **ballistics** and **DNA** evidence. They must understand how to use equipment to gather evidence. For example, agents use ultraviolet light at crime scenes to detect invisible blood spots and fingerprints.

Bank robberies and murders are just a few of the crimes that agents investigate.  In such cases, FBI agents must protect the evidence from outsiders.  Agents take photographs of the scene.  They interview witnesses and take notes.  They gather evidence and

## The Hoover Era

J. Edgar Hoover (1895 – 1972) was one of the most important people in FBI history.  The Justice Department hired Hoover as a spy catcher in 1917.  He remained with the agency and became its director in 1924.

J. Edgar Hoover

Hoover improved how crimes were investigated. He started the FBI crime lab and the program of collecting fingerprints. Hoover also organized a formal training program for FBI agents that later became the FBI Academy.

Hoover was FBI director for forty-eight years. Late in his career, some people began to criticize him.  They thought he held office for too long and had too much power.  Since Hoover, the FBI director's term has been limited to ten years.

prepare it for further study at crime labs. Afterward, a report is made. Other evidence, such as fingerprints, will be run through the FBI's database to find matches. Working on a criminal investigation takes time and patience. Agents are trained to examine every detail.

Carrying heavy protective gear, an FBI SWAT team trains for high-risk missions.

# SWAT Teams

Like state and local police departments, the FBI has SWAT (Special Weapons and Tactics) teams. These FBI agents are trained to handle high-risk situations. They may be called in to arrest heavily armed criminals. Sometimes they protect important people such as presidents. In rare cases, they may be used to control crowds during riots.

# Hostage Rescue Teams

Some FBI agents are members of hostage rescue teams (HRTs). These agents are specially trained to rescue hostages. They may also be called in to fight possible terror plots.

Most members have backgrounds in **psychology**. Some are foreign language experts. They have knowledge of human behavior, helping them understand how criminals act. HRTs must be good at reasoning with criminals to prevent the loss of lives.

## Cold Cases

Some cases take a very long time to solve. These unsolved cases are called "cold" because the evidence has provided few leads. Sometimes, unexpected details come out years after a crime was committed. In these instances, agents working in special units of the FBI will reopen the case.

# CHAPTER 3

# GETTING THE JOB DONE

Thousands of people work at FBI headquarters in Washington, D.C. But most FBI employees work elsewhere.

New agents are sent to one of the bureau's fifty-six **field offices**. These offices are located in major cities throughout the United States. New agents can ask to work in a particular city. But the FBI gets the final say. Agents are sent where they are most needed.

## At Home and Overseas

The bureau has many smaller offices. These offices are called **resident agencies**. They are located in more than 400 small cities and towns. Each resident agency is attached to a field office.

In addition, the bureau has agents in more than sixty foreign countries. Some of these agents aid local police. Others work to protect American lives and property. In August 1998, terrorists in Africa bombed two U.S. **embassies**. The blasts in Kenya and Tanzania killed 263 people. More than 5,500 others were injured. The FBI sent agents to both countries to help find the people who planned the attack.

The FBI headquarters building in Washington, D.C., is named for J. Edgar Hoover.

# High-Tech Gear

Fighting terrorism takes more than careful police work. FBI agents protect the public with the most advanced firearms and safety equipment. Some agents need full-body armor, night-vision goggles, and armored vehicles. They have the help of outside scientists who provide information, such as how to disarm a bomb.

# On the Job: Agent Laurie J. Bennett

Laurie Bennett grew up on a dairy farm in Green Bay, Wisconsin, with her eight brothers and sisters. Before joining the FBI, she served in the U.S. Army. In Georgia, Bennett taught fitness to police officers and firefighters. She signed on with the FBI in 1990. In 1996, the FBI sent her to Saudi Arabia to investigate a bombing in which nineteen U.S. airmen were killed. She has also worked on other terrorism cases. In 2006, she was named to head the FBI field office in Buffalo, New York.

## Crime Labs

In 1932, the FBI began using crime labs to collect and study crime data around the country. Today, the FBI has more than 40 million sets of fingerprints in its computers. In minutes, computers can match prints found at a crime scene with those of a known criminal.

FBI crime labs can also inspect traces of evidence, such as bits of cloth, fibers, and hairs, with high-powered microscopes. Other experts may examine the handwriting in a note or letter that was found at a crime scene. Even the smallest bits of evidence can help crack a case.

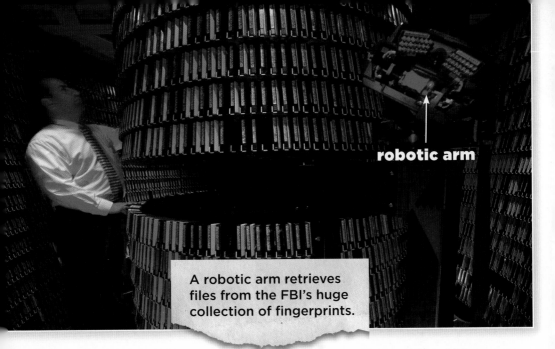

robotic arm

A robotic arm retrieves files from the FBI's huge collection of fingerprints.

## Busted!

In the early 1930s, many criminals became famous. Some had colorful names like "Pretty Boy" Floyd and "Machine Gun" Kelly. Bonnie Parker and Clyde Barrow were robbers and killers. But Bonnie and Clyde were also media stars. So was John Dillinger. Each crime his gang committed made huge headlines.

To fight these famous crooks, Congress gave the FBI new powers. For the first time, agents got the right to carry guns. In June 1934, J. Edgar Hoover called Dillinger "Public Enemy Number One." A month later, federal agents killed Dillinger in Chicago.

# CHAPTER 4

# BECOMING AN AGENT

**B**ecoming an FBI agent is difficult. When hiring new agents, the bureau sets very high standards. You must meet strict requirements before you can qualify for an FBI job. The bureau will do a complete background check on you. You must also complete a tough training program.

Students at the FBI Academy in Quantico, Virginia, learn the right technique for taking down a suspect.

A college student talks to an FBI recruiter at a University of Southern Mississippi job fair.

# Meeting Standards

You must answer "yes" to all the following questions before the FBI will even consider hiring you as a special agent:

- Are you a U.S. citizen?
- Are you at least twenty-three years old?
- Do you have a four-year college degree?
- Do you have a driver's license?
- Can you go anywhere the FBI needs to send you?

These questions are only the beginning. You must have good eyesight and hearing. You must be able to pass a physical fitness test. You must also have some skill the FBI needs. For example, the FBI needs people with training in law and **accounting**. Several years of police work may be helpful. So is military experience.

# The Next Step — A Background Check

FBI agents have a lot of responsibility. They can look at top-secret files. They carry guns. They are trained to use deadly force. The FBI needs to be sure its agents will not abuse their powers.

Before you can work as a special agent, the FBI will examine your character. Agents will ask your friends and teachers about you. You'll need to pass a lie detector test. You'll need to pass a drug test, too.

Good FBI agents must have high moral standards. To qualify for the FBI, you'll need a clean record. No serious crimes. No drugs. No bad debts.

All trainees at the FBI Academy must take a lie detector test.

# Wanted: Accountants!

The FBI deals with many crimes involving money. Some crooks are very skilled at moving money around. FBI agents need to find the money — *and* catch the crooks who try to hide it. That is why the government needs agents who know accounting.

Here is a well-known case. Al "Scarface" Capone was a famous crime boss in the 1920s. His gang committed many violent crimes. Capone served prison time in the 1930s. Why? Because he failed to pay federal taxes on the money his gang made. The accountants battled Scarface — and the accountants won!

# The FBI Academy

The next big step in becoming a special agent is the New Agents' Training Unit. "New Agent Trainees" are called NATs. Training takes place at the FBI Academy in Quantico, Virginia. For seventeen weeks, the NATs practice field exercises, study training manuals, and improve their physical fitness.

NATs spend much of their time in classrooms. They learn how to interview witnesses. They practice how to question suspects. Law is an important subject. So is learning the right way to enforce the law. NATs must pass nine separate exams on classroom subjects.

Work outside the classroom is also tough. NATs practice with pistols and other guns. They are tested on the accuracy of their shooting. NATs are trained to defend themselves. They learn how to control, search, and handcuff suspects. They practice boxing. They learn how to take away someone's weapon — and how to keep control of their own. NATs must pass a test in defensive tactics. NATs also must pass several physical fitness tests.

NATs who complete their training must then pledge to follow the FBI's core values. NATs pledge to obey the U.S. Constitution.

Target practice is an important part of FBI training at Quantico.

FBI trainees show off their street smarts when arresting a suspect at Hogan's Alley, a mock town built for training at the FBI Academy.

# Hogan's Alley

The last test NATs must pass at Quantico is given at Hogan's Alley. Here, NATs put all their training and study into practice. Hogan's Alley looks like part of a city. A "crime" has been committed. Can the NATs solve it? They talk with witnesses. They confront suspects. They defend themselves against attackers. In Hogan's Alley, NATs show they can deal with the real world.

# CHAPTER 5
# MEETING NEW THREATS

FBI agents enforce more than 260 federal laws. The FBI became famous for cracking down on bank robbers and killers. But federal laws target many other types of crimes. For example, it is illegal to pollute the air, water, or soil. The FBI has squads of agents to catch people who poison the environment. Agents also crack down on some of today's biggest threats — fighting terrorism and computer crimes.

The FBI launched a search for terrorist leader Osama (or Usama) bin Laden after terrorists destroyed the World Trade Center (right) in 2001.

## Fighting Terrorism

Terrorists struck the United States on September 11, 2001. Nearly three thousand people were killed. Most of the deaths came at the World Trade Center in New York City. Other victims died in Virginia and Pennsylvania.

# On the Job: Agent J. Douglas Kouns

J. Douglas Kouns is an FBI agent who recently finished an assignment in Washington, D.C. He worked for the FBI division that protects the public from terrorists. Some terrorists have tried to use chemical weapons. Kouns knows a lot about these kinds of weapons because he studied chemistry in college. He recommends that students interested in careers in the FBI set themselves apart by learning a language. He encourages young people to set realistic goals. "We will all make mistakes," says Kouns. "What makes us successful is how we deal with them."

Law enforcement officials set up this computer lab in Dallas, Texas, to combat cyber crime.

The attacks shocked America — and the world. They also forced FBI leaders to do some hard thinking. Could the FBI have prevented the attacks? No one knew for sure. But one thing was certain. Like other U.S. agencies, the bureau knew it would need to do a better job. The top job of FBI agents is to protect the United States from terrorists.

# Cyber Crime

Another growing focus of the FBI is solving computer crime, also called **cyber crime**. Cyber crime takes many forms. One type of cyber crime is called **phishing**. That's when crooks put together a fake web site that looks like a real one people know. People are encouraged to go to that site and type in their credit

## Other Federal Crime Fighters

The FBI is not the only federal crime-fighting agency. Here are some others:

- *Drug Enforcement Administration (DEA)*: Enforces federal drug laws. Tries to stop illegal drugs from coming into the country.
- *Bureau of Alcohol, Tobacco, Firearms and Explosives (ATF)*: Enforces federal gun laws. Acts to stop illegal buying and selling of alcohol or tobacco products.
- *U.S. Secret Service*: Protects the president and other top U.S. officials. Enforces laws against **counterfeiting**.

# The FBI Seal

The FBI seal explains the bureau's history and mission. Do you notice the circle of thirteen stars? They stand for the original thirteen states. The red stripes? They mean strength and courage. The white stripes? They suggest truth and light. The scales above the stripes stand for justice, as does the color blue.

The seal contains the FBI motto: *Fidelity, Bravery, Integrity*. Each of the three words starts with one of the letters in FBI. *Fidelity* means being faithful or loyal. *Integrity* means being honest.

card number. The criminals collect the credit card numbers. They then use the numbers themselves or sell them to other criminals. FBI agents are working hard to crack down on phishing.

**Hackers** also pose a serious problem. Today, all big companies rely on computer systems. Governments do, too. Some hackers act like cyber terrorists. They tap into these systems and steal valuable data. They also attack these systems and try to shut them down. Stopping cyber crime is one of the biggest jobs FBI agents face today.

# FBI AGENT

## OUTLOOK

- More than 30,000 people work for the FBI. More than 12,000 are special agents.
- The FBI needs more agents. But standards are high, and competition is very tough.

## WHAT YOU'LL DO

- Your main job will be to enforce federal law and to protect the United States by investigating and fighting crime.
- As a new agent, you'll be sent to one of the FBI's fifty-six field offices, located in major U.S. cities.
- Every day is different. Some days, you'll be working at a desk. Other days you'll be out in the field looking for clues and catching crooks.

## WHAT YOU'LL NEED

- A four-year college degree is required. You must be at least twenty-three years old and in good physical shape.
- The FBI will do a thorough background check on you. You must have a clean record. You will also need to pass a lie detector test and a drug test.

## WHAT YOU'LL EARN

- Agents get a starting salary of between $61,100 and $69,900 a year. Experienced agents may earn up to $100,000 or more.

Source: FBI

# GLOSSARY

**accounting** — a system for keeping and analyzing financial records

**ballistics** — the study of how bullets move and what happens to them as they are fired

**counterfeiting** — a crime in which something fake, such as fake money, is passed off as real

**cyber crime** — crime related to computers

**DNA** — a substance found in all living things that determines their traits

**embassies** — buildings where government employees carry out their official duties in foreign countries

**evidence** — the information gathered at a crime scene, such as fingerprints

**FBI** — stands for Federal Bureau of Investigation; an agency of the U.S. government that solves crimes that break federal laws

**field offices** — fifty-six main FBI offices located in U.S. cities

**hackers** — people who use computers to gain illegal access to other computer systems

**hostage** — a person taken and held by force

**notorious** — widely known for doing bad things

**phishing** — a type of Internet fraud

**psychology** — the study of the mind and human behavior

**resident agencies** — more than 400 FBI offices in U.S. cities and towns; also called "satellite" offices

**serial killer** — a criminal who, over time, murders several people in a similar way

**surveillance** — watching someone or something, often while trying not to be seen

**terrorists** — people who use violence to force other people or governments to meet certain demands

# TO FIND OUT MORE

## Books

*Crime Scene Investigator.* Cool Careers: Adventure Careers (series). Geoffrey M. Horn (Gareth Stevens, 2008)

*FBI Agent.* Virtual Apprentice (series). Gail Karlitz (Ferguson Publishing, 2008)

*Law Enforcement.* Discovering Careers for Your Future (series). (Ferguson Publishing, 2008)

*Special Agent and Careers in the FBI.* Homeland Security and Counterterrorism Careers (series). Ann Gaines (Enslow Publishers, 2006)

*Working in Law Enforcement.* My Future Career (series). William David Thomas (Gareth Stevens, 2005)

## Web Sites

**FBI Academy**
*www.fbi.gov/hq/td/academy/academy.htm*
Discover everything you need to know about the school where FBI agents are trained.

**Federal Bureau of Investigation: Careers**
*www.fbijobs.gov*
Search for detailed information about FBI jobs, and learn why people joined the FBI.

**Federal Bureau of Investigation: Kids' Page**
*www.fbi.gov/fbikids.htm*
Learn how the FBI does its work, including a day in the life of a special agent.

# INDEX

# About the Author

Geoffrey M. Horn has written more than three dozen books for young people and adults, along with hundreds of articles for encyclopedias and other works. He lives in southwestern Virginia, in the foothills of the Blue Ridge Mountains, with his wife, their collie, and six cats. He dedicates this book to all those who fight crime the right way, while honoring basic American freedoms.